Engelsgrube
Bewohner
mit Parkausweis E
frei

Lübeck
Kulturerbe der Welt
World's Cultural Heritage

Lübeck ist Kultur. Das Holstentor

Lübeck is culture. The Holstentor

Lübeck

Kulturerbe der Welt

World's Cultural Heritage

Klaus J. Groth und Dirk Hourticolon

SCHMIDT RÖMHILD

Inhalt

Contents

Bibliografische Information der Deutschen Nationalbibliothek

Die Deutsche Nationalbibliothek verzeichnet diese Publikation in der Deutschen Nationalbibliografie; detaillierte bibliografische Daten sind im Internet über http://dnb.d-nb.de abrufbar.

Text und Konzeption: Klaus J. Groth

Fotos: Dirk Hourticolon, Olaf Timm (S. 2), W. Maxiwat (S. 6-7), Theater Lübeck (S. 24), Passatchor (S. 70), Christine Silz (S. 102)

Gestaltung: Atelier Schmidt-Römhild, Lübeck

Gesamtherstellung: Schmidt-Römhild, Lübeck

ISBN-13: 978-3-7950-1278-6

ISBN-10: 3-7950-1278-3

Lübecker
Theater

Von Wasser umschlossen: Lübecks Altstadt liegt auf einer Insel

Surrounded by water: Lübeck's Altstadt is situated on an island

Das 1284 erbaute Heiligen-Geist-Hospital gilt als das älteste Altenheim der Welt

Lübeck ist Kultur

Kultur ist kein Teil von Lübeck, Lübeck ist Kultur. Zugegeben, das scheint eine etwas gewagte Behauptung zu sein. Wer sie aufstellt, muss umgehend den Nachweis erbringen. Bitte, gerne:

Als erste Stadt Deutschlands wurde Lübeck 1987 in die Liste des Weltkulturerbes der UNESCO aufgenommen. Die so ausgezeichnete historische Altstadt wird heute in einem Atemzug mit Venedig, Florenz und Brügge genannt. Die nordische Backsteingotik präsentiert sich nirgendwo so eindrucksvoll und geschlossen

wie in Lübeck. Die himmelweisende Silhouette der sieben Kirchtürme auf dem Stadthügel, die prächtigen Häuser der Bürger und die anheimelnden Häuschen der Gänge und Höfe, der unveränderte mittelalterliche Grundriss der Straßenzüge auf der Stadtinsel – das alles sucht seinesgleichen. Mehr als 800 Häuser auf der Stadtinsel stehen unter Denkmalschutz. Sie bilden ein geschlossenes, harmonisches Ensemble, dessen stilistische Ausdrucksformen von der Gotik über Renaissance und Barock bis zum Klassizismus reichen. Zur Straßenfront stehen die imposanten Häuser der Kaufleute und Handwerker, gewissermaßen in deren Windschatten ducken sich in den Gängen die bescheidenen Häuser und Buden der kleinen Leute. Häuser in Lübeck – das ist lebendige Sozialgeschichte. Dies einmalige Stadtbild veranlasste die UNESCO zur Begründung ihrer Entscheidung: „Die Eintragung in diese Liste (des Weltkulturerbes, d. A.) zeichnet den allumfassenden außergewöhnlichen Wert von Lübeck aus, der zum Wohle der gesamten Menschheit gefördert werden muss."

Profane und sakrale Bauten, Wohnhäuser und Gotteshäuser, sie sind gewissermaßen die Hardware.

The Heiligen-Geist-Hospital, built in 1284, is the oldest retirement home in the world

Lübeck is culture

Culture isn't just part of Lübeck – Lübeck is culture. Admittedly this may sound like something of a bold statement, and one that shouldn't be made without good cause.

By way of justification: in 1987, Lübeck became the first city in Germany to be included on the list of UNESCO World Heritage Sites. Thanks to that recognition, the old town of Lübeck is now mentioned in the same breath as Venice, Florence and Bruges. Nowhere in the world will you find a more remarkably complete example of the northern German Backstein Gothic style. The silhouettes of the seven church spires, pointing to the heavens from the hill; the splendid patrician residences and the quaint little houses lining the alleyways and courtyards; the course traced by the roads on the island, unchanged since medieval times – all of this is quite unique. On the island where the old town is situated, the 800 houses listed under preservation orders make up a compact and harmonious ensemble that traces stylistic developments from Gothic to Renaissance, from Baroque to Classical. Streets are lined with the imposing houses of the merchants and traders, somewhat overshadowing the more modest dwellings and workshops of ordinary people, tucked away in the lanes. The houses of Lübeck therefore offer a living social commentary, a matchless

Backsteingiebel aus allen Epochen prägen das unverwechselbare Bild der Stadt

Decorative brickwork gables in a variety of styles capture the unique ambience of the city

Die Software ist das kulturelle Leben in der Stadt. Oder wie es Thomas Mann in einem Aufsatz formulierte: „Lübeck als geistige Lebensform". Sie umfasst das große kulturelle Erbe und gegenwärtige Kulturpflege gleichermaßen.

Überhaupt Thomas Mann. Er rechnete Lübeck zu den „besseren Herkünften", obgleich das Verhältnis zu seiner Vaterstadt durch erhebliche Spannungen geprägt war. Die Lübecker verübelten ihm lange Zeit, dass der Dichter ihnen mit dem Roman „Buddenbrooks" einen Spiegel vorgehalten hatte, der sie nicht gerade vorteilhaft aussehen ließ. Die Anerkennung der Weltgeltung des Dichters durch die Verleihung des Literatur-Nobelpreises 1929 versöhnte zwar noch nicht alle, aber viele. Heute sind die Lübecker ausgesprochen stolz auf diesen Sohn der Stadt.

Seit Günter Grass der Literatur-Nobelpreis 1999 durch die schwedische Akademie zugesprochen wurde, darf sich Lübeck als Stadt der zwei Literatur-Nobelpreisträger bezeichnen. Günter Grass ist zugleich der dritte Träger eines Nobelpreises mit enger Verbindung zu Lübeck. 1971 hatte der in Lübeck geborene Willy Brandt den Friedensnobelpreis in Empfang genommen.

Den beiden Trägern des Literatur-Nobelpreises sind in Lübeck eigene Literatur-Häuser gewidmet; ein Erinnerungs- und Forschungszentrum für den Friedensnobelpreisträger Willy Brandt kommt hinzu (Königstraße 21). Das ältere Literaturhaus ist das „Heinrich- und Thomas-Mann-Zentrum" (Mengstraße 4) im Buddenbrook-Haus, das heute zu den besonders häufig besuchten kulturellen Einrichtungen der Stadt zählt. Das Günter-Grass-Haus (Glockengießerstraße 21) mit einer reichhaltigen Ausstellung des grafischen Werks des Künstlers dient zugleich als Sekretariat des Schriftstellers.

Zum eigenen Literaturhaus hat es ein weiterer Dichter Lübecks nicht gebracht, obgleich er zu Lebzeiten nicht weniger Anerkennung fand: Emanuel Geibel. In der Reihe beachtenswerter Literaten, die Lübeck hervorbrachte, ist sein Name auf einem der vorderen Plätze zu nennen. Seine Gedichtbände erlebten bis zu 100 Auflagen. Den Zeitgenossen klangen sie wie Musik, nur die Gedichte von Goethe und Heine wurden häufiger vertont als die Geibels. Heute ist davon ein Lied geblieben, das nahezu jeder kennt: „Der Mai ist gekommen…".

Eine der bekanntesten Adressen der Welt: Das Buddenbrookhaus in der Mengstraße 4

One of the most well-known addresses worldwide: Buddenbrookhaus in Mengstrasse 4

Im Zeichen des Butts: Garten des Günter-Grass-Hauses in der Glockengießerstraße

Under the sign of the flounder: the garden of the Günter-Grass-Haus in Glockengiesserstrasse

Ein Literaturhaus – auch für die Bildende Kunst: Ausstellung im Günter-Grass-Haus

A house of art and literature: exhibition in Günter-Grass-Haus

townscape that prompted UNESCO to justify its decision by declaring: "The inclusion on the list [of World Heritage Sites] reflects the generally outstanding value of Lübeck that must be promoted to the benefit of humankind in general."

Secular and sacred structures, residential buildings and houses of God – these may be thought of as the 'hardware'; the cultural life of the city is the 'software'. Or as Thomas Mann put it in one of his essays, Lübeck is a 'spiritual life form'. The city lends equal prominence to its glorious cultural heritage and the modern-day need to uphold that culture.

But let's stay with Thomas Mann. Although his relationship with his home town was marked by considerable tensions, he counted Lübeck "among the better places to come from". For a long time, the people of Lübeck resented Mann for his novel 'Buddenbrooks', which held up a mirror that didn't show them in a particularly positive light. When the poet was awarded

Wo einst die Koggen festmachten: Traditionsschiffe im Oldtimerhafen der Trave

Wer sich in Lübeck auf die Spuren der Schriftsteller und Dichter begibt, entdeckt Erstaunliches. Neben Köln war Lübeck die wichtigste Stadt des Buchdrucks im deutschsprachigen Raum. Zahlreiche Veröffentlichungen des ausgehenden Mittelalters wurden hier verlegt: „Dat narren schvp" (1497), „Lübecker Bilderbibel" (1494), „Henselyns boek" (1498), „Reynke de Vos" (1498). Da ist es kaum verwunderlich, dass das älteste Verlags- und Druckhaus Deutschlands in Lübeck beheimatet ist. Die Geschichte des Verlages Schmidt-Römhild reicht bis 1579 zurück, und er ist heute produktiver denn je. Das Unternehmen des Druckers Johannes Ballhorn (gestorben 1573) überdauerte eine derartige Zeitspanne nicht. Dafür aber ging sein Name in den allgemeinen deutschen Sprachgebrauch ein. „Verballhornen" wird heute jenes Missgeschick genannt, bei der Korrektur von Fehlern neue Fehler zu

Seine Gedichte wurden zu Liedern: Emanuel Geibel schrieb „Der Mai ist gekommen…"

His poems were put to music: Emanuel Geibel created the popular song "May has come..."

Where great cogs once moored: traditional vessels in the old-timer port on the River Trave

the 1929 Nobel Prize in Literature, thus acknowledging his international standing, many (but not all) were placated. Today, the city takes an unreserved pride in this son of Lübeck.

In 1999, the Swedish Academy conferred the Nobel Prize in Literature on Günter Grass, at the same time confirming Lübeck as a city of two literary Nobel Prize winners. Günter Grass was actually the third person with close connections to the city to be awarded such a distinction: in 1971 Willy Brandt, who was born in Lübeck, received the Nobel Peace Prize.

Special literary houses are devoted to both of Lübeck's Nobel Laureates in Literature; there is also an exhibition and research centre dedicated to Nobel Peace Laureate Willy Brandt at Königstrasse 21. The first literary house to be established was the Heinrich and Thomas Mann Centre (within the Buddenbrooks House at Mengstrasse 4); today it ranks as one of the city's most popular cultural attractions. The Günter Grass House (Glockengiesserstrasse 21) features an extensive collection of his graphic artworks and also serves as an office for the writer.

However, there is no literary house devoted to another Lübeck poet who achieved similar levels of reverence during his lifetime. The name Emanuel Geibel must feature highly on any list of noteworthy literary figures that Lübeck has produced; his volumes of poetry have gone through around 100 editions. To his contemporaries, the work of Geibel had a musical resonance; only the poems of Goethe and Heine have been set to music more often. Today, almost everyone is

Der doppelköpfige Adler, das Zeichen der freien Hansestadt

The double-headed eagle, symbol of the Free City of the Hanseatic League

Das Schleswig-Holstein Musik Festival ist in Lübeck zuhause. Hier werden die großen Konzerte geplant und organisiert

Schleswig-Holstein's music festival has found a home in Lübeck. This is where large concerts are planned and organized

produzieren. Sogar in den Duden wurde dies Synonym für eine Verschlimmbesserung aufgenommen.

Lübeck und die Musik, das ein weiteres, besonders schönes Kapitel in der Kulturgeschichte der Stadt. Und der Gegenwart. Lübeck ist eine Stadt der Musik, der Kirchenmusik insbesondere. Der Komponist und Organist Dietrich Buxtehude (1637-1707) zog in der Marienkirche 39 Jahre lang alle Register. Er setzte die von seinem Vorgänger begründeten Abendmusiken in der Kirche fort – eine Tradition, die übrigens bis heute fortlebt. Johann Sebastian Bach und Georg Friedrich Händel pilgerten nach Lübeck, um dem Spiel

familiar with the song "Der Mai ist gekommen" ("May has come").

Anyone who comes to Lübeck to follow in the footsteps of writers and poets can expect to make some amazing discoveries. After Cologne, Lübeck was the most important city for letterpress printing in the German-speaking region. As the Middle Ages drew to a close, numerous books were published here, including 'Dat narren schvp' (1497), the Lübeck illustrated bible of 1494, 'Henselyns boek' (1498) and 'Reynke de Vos' (1498). It is no surprise to find that Schmidt-Römhild, Germany's oldest printing and publishing house, is

Im Sommer klingt Schleswig-Holstein klassisch. Vor allem die „Musik auf dem Lande" während des Festivals findet immer neue Freunde (Foto unten: Schloss Emkendorf)

For the summer music festival, Schleswig-Holstein goes classic. Very popular: concerts presented in rural locations (below: Schloss Emkendorf)

In jeder Tonlage stilvoll:
Im Innenhof der Musikhochschule

Always a stylish note: the courtyard of the College of Music

des großen Meisters zu lauschen. In der langen Liste der bedeutenden Organisten der Stadt ist noch ein Name auf vorderem Rang zu nennen: Hugo August Distler (1908-1942). Er wirkte an der Jakobikirche und hinterließ ein umfangreiches Werk kirchlicher Chormusik, aber auch weltliche Kantaten und Klaviermusik.

In der Musikhochschule wird heute die lange musikalische Tradition an junge Musiker aus aller Welt weitergegeben. Hinter den alten Fassaden in der Großen Petersgrube, in der mehr als 20 unter Denkmalschutz stehende Kaufmannshäuser zur Hochschule zusammengefasst wurden, und in der ebenfalls denkmalgeschützten Holstentorhalle erklingt heute Musik von der Klassik bis zur Moderne. Angegliedert ist das Brahms-Institut, das mittlerweile eine führende Rolle in der europäischen Forschung über Leben und Schaffen des Komponisten Johannes Brahms übernommen hat. Und schließlich

Hinter den Fassaden schöner alter Patrizierhäuser unterrichtet die Musikhochschule in modern gestalteten Räumen

The College of Music instructs up-and-coming musicians in modern facilities, hiding behind the façades of magnificent patrician homes

located in Lübeck. The company, which is more productive today than ever before, can trace its history back to 1579. The business founded by the printer Johannes Ballhorn (died 1573) did not survive for such a long time. His name has passed into common parlance in Germany: today, the word "Verballhornen" applies to any mishap whereby an attempt to correct an error produces new errors. The Duden dictionary even lists the term as a synonym for 'disimprovement'.

Another particularly rewarding aspect of the city's cultural past (and present) is the connection between Lübeck and music. Lübeck is a city of music, particularly church music. For 39 years, composer and organist Dietrich Buxtehude (1637-1707) literally pulled out all

ist noch das Schleswig-Holstein Musik Festival zu nennen. Alljährlich füllt es mit seinen Aufführungen Konzertsäle, Kirchen und Scheunen im ganzen Land zwischen den Meeren. Gelenkt wird das Festival von Lübeck aus, denn hier hat es seinen Sitz in dem hervorragend sanierten Rantzau Palais.

In der Hansezeit war Lübeck eine reiche Stadt. Sie bot auch den bildenden Künstlern ein sicheres Auskommen. So ist es nicht verwunderlich, dass sich der Name der Stadt mit denen bekannter Maler und Schnitzer verbindet. Arbeiten des 15. und 16. Jahrhunderts von Bernt Notke, Henning van der Heide

the stops at St. Mary's Church. He brought the 'evening music' pioneered by his forebears to the church – a tradition that survives to this day. Johann Sebastian Bach and Georg Friedrich Händel made a pilgrimage to Lübeck to hear the great master play. Another prominent name on the long list of the city's leading organists is Hugo August Distler (1908-1942), who served at the church of Saint Jacob. He bequeathed a vast body of ecclesiastical choral music as well as more secular cantatas and piano music.

Today, this long musical tradition is handed down to young musicians from around the world at the Academy

Drei auf einen Blick (von links): Jakobikirche, Burgtor, Marienkirche

A proud view (from the left): St. Jacob's Church, Burgtor, St. Mary's Church

Der römische Krieger auf der Puppenbrücke soll die Bürgertugenden verkörpern. So dachte man sich das 1776

Created in 1776, the Roman warrior on Puppenbrücke was to symbolize the virtues of the bourgeoisie

Die alten Speicher an der Trave erzählen noch von der Zeit, als die Handelsschiffe in die Stadt kamen

The old storehouses on the Trave bear witness to a time when trading vessels still moored in Lübeck

Kluge und törichte Jungfern – Sandsteinfiguren im St.-Annen-Museum (um 1400)

Wise and foolish maidens – sandstone sculpture in St.-Annen-Museum (around 1400)

oder Hermen Rode gehören überall im Ostseeraum zu den Glanzpunkten in Kirchen und Klöstern. Dass diese Künstler besonders zahlreich in Lübeck vertreten sind, versteht sich von selbst.

Der Lübecker Maler Friedrich Overbeck (1789 –1869) und der von ihm in Rom gebildete Kreis der „Nazarener“ erlebt in jüngster Zeit gerade eine Neuentdeckung. Einige der schönsten Bilder Overbecks werden im Behnhaus gezeigt. Dort hängen auch Gemälde des Norwegers Edvard Munch (1863 –1944), der in einer seiner schwersten Lebenskrisen Zuflucht bei einem Förderer in Lübeck fand. Weitsichtige Unterstützung fand auch der Bildhauer Ernst Barlach (1870–1938) in Lübeck, und das in einer Zeit, in der ihm die allgemeine und offizielle Anerkennung verweigert wurde. Seine Figurengruppe „Gemeinschaft der Heiligen“ steht auf der Westseite der Katharinenkirche.

Eine Stadt, die in so reichem Maße mit den Zeugnissen künstlerischen Schaffens ausgestattet ist, müsste über

Blick vom Malerwinkel: Im Vordergrund die Musikhochschule, dahinter die Türme von Sankt Marien und Sankt Petri

View from Malerwinkel. In the foreground the College of Music; in the background the church towers of St. Mary's and St. Peter's

of Music. Musical styles ranging from classical to modern emanate from behind the ancient façades along Grosse Petersgrube, where over 20 listed merchant houses were amalgamated to form the Academy, as well as the Holstentorhalle, similarly under a preservation order. Also affiliated is the Brahms Institute, which now assumes a leading role in European research into the life and work of the composer Johannes Brahms. Finally, there is the annual Schleswig-Holstein Music Festival, whose performances fill concert halls, churches and country halls across the state that lies between the North Sea and the Baltic. The festival is run from the beautifully renovated Rantzau Palais in Lübeck.

Mittelalterliche Altäre zeigt das Sankt-Annen-Museum in einmaliger Zahl. Foto: Rosenkranzaltar (um 1525) aus dem Heiligen-Geist-Hospital

The Sankt-Annen-Museum shows a unique collection of medieval altars. Photograph: Altar of the Garland of Roses (around 1525) from the Heiligen-Geist-Hospital

Diele eines Kaufmannshauses aus dem 18. Jahrhundert im St.-Annen-Museum

Hall in a merchant's house dating back to the 18th century, reconstructed in St.-Annen-Museum

herausragende Museen und Ausstellungsflächen verfügen. Lübeck hat sie:

An erster Stelle ist das **St.-Annen-Museum** zu nennen. Das ehemalige Kloster bietet nicht nur einen grandiosen Rahmen für die Präsentation einer einmaligen Sammlung mittelalterlicher Altäre, Holzskulpturen und Tafelmalereien, es besitzt auch eine überaus reizvolle Sammlung von Kinderspielzeug.

Die neue **Kunsthalle** am St.-Annen-Museum zeigt zeitgenössische Kunst.

Im **Holstentor** wird die große Zeit der Hanse lebendig.

In den alten Kaufmannshäusern **Behnhaus/ Drägerhaus** wird Kunst des 20. Jahrhunderts gezeigt, unter anderem von Friedrich Overbeck, Caspar David Friedrich, Max Liebermann, Lovis Corinth und Edvard Munch.

Triptychon des Greveradenaltars, 1491 von Hans Memling geschaffen. Ehemals im Dom, jetzt im St.-Annen-Museum

Triptych of the Greverade altar, created by Hans Memling in 1491. Transferred from the cathedral to St.-Annen-Museum

1502 wurde mit dem Bau des Sankt-Annen-Klosters begonnen, heute ist es eines der schönsten Museen

Construction work on the Convent of St. Annen began in 1502; today it is home to one of the most beautiful museums

In the age of the Hanse, Lübeck was a wealthy town where even artists could make a good living. It is no surprise, therefore, that the name Lübeck became associated with famous painters and woodcarvers. Works produced by Bernt Notke, Henning van der Heide and Hermen Rode in the 15th and 16th centuries grace churches and monasteries throughout the Baltic region. Needless to say, the work of these artists is particularly well represented in Lübeck.

The Lübeck painter Friedrich Overbeck (1789-1869) and the 'Nazarenes', the group of artists he brought together in Rome, were rediscovered in recent times. A number of Overbeck's finest works are now displayed in the Behnhaus art museum alongside paintings by the Norwegian Edvard Munch (1863–1944), who sought refuge with a patron in Lübeck at the most difficult times of his life. The sculptor Ernst Barlach (1870–1938) also found far-sighted support in Lübeck at a time when he had been refused general and official recognition. His group of figures depicting a community of the Saints ('Gemeinschaft der Heiligen') can be seen on the western façade of the church of Saint Catharine.

Das **Burgkloster** zeigt eindrucksvoll die Welt des hansischen Kaufmanns.

Im **Beichthaus** am Burgkloster werden Fundstücke der Lübecker Archäologie ausgestellt.

Damit ist die Aufzählung der Lübecker Museen und Ausstellungen längst nicht komplett. Zu nennen sind noch das Museum für Natur und Umwelt, die Völkerkundesammlung, die Katharinenkirche und die St.-Petri-Kirche mit wechselnden Ausstellungen, die Geschichtswerkstatt in der ehemaligen Metallhütte und schließlich – nicht nur für Kinder ein Sympathieträger ersten Ranges – das Museum für Puppentheater mit mehr als 20 000 Objekten aus der ganzen Welt.

Kultur in Lübeck, das sind auch das Städtische Schauspiel und die Oper mit einem wunderschönen

Kunst für die Kunst: Bühnenvorhang nach einem Entwurf des Jugendstil-Architekten Martin Dülfer

A piece of art created for the theatre: stage curtains following a design by the Art Nouveau architect Martin Dülfer

Ein Schmuckstück des Jugendstil: Theatersaal im Großen Haus der Städtischen Bühnen

A jewel in the Art Nouveau crown: auditorium in the Grosses Haus der Städtischen Bühnen theatre

Ein wahrer Musentempel: das 1908 erbaute Theater der Stadt

Where thespians reign supreme: the city's theatre built in 1908

Inevitably, a city with the rich artistic legacy of Lübeck will boast excellent museums and exhibition spaces. Foremost among these is the ***St. Annen museum****. This former monastery provides a grand showcase for a unique collection of medieval altars, wooden sculptures and panel paintings as well as a delightful collection of toys.*

The ***Kunsthalle*** *art gallery, which adjoins the St. Annen museum, is devoted to contemporary art.*

The glory of the Hanseatic League era is brought back to life at the ***Holstentor****.*

The old merchant houses making up the ***Behnhaus/ Drägerhaus museum*** *now house 20th century art,*

Seit 1994 ein Zentrum der Kultur in Lübeck: die von Meinhardt von Gerkan entworfene Musik- und Kongreßhalle

Lübeck centre of culture since 1994: the music and congress hall designed by Meinhardt von Gerkan

Theater im Jugendstil, das Städtische Symphonieorchester, die Nordischen Filmtage mit Produktionen der nordischen Länder, die zahlreichen Gastspiele in der Musik- und Kongreßhalle, die Junge Oper als Experimentierfeld für junge Darsteller, das Junge Kammerorchester, die Media Docks in einem ehemaligen Hafenspeicher, die zahlreichen kleinen Theater.

Kultur in Lübeck, das ist so vieles. Und darum ist die eingangs aufgestellte Feststellung nicht zu vollmundig: Kultur ist kein Teil von Lübeck, Lübeck ist Kultur.

Freier Blick über die Stadt: Figurengruppe „Die Fremden" von Thomas Schütte auf dem Dach der Musik- und Kongreßhalle

Gazing across the city: "The Strangers", group of sculptures on the roof of the music and congress hall, created by Thomas Schütte

including works by Friedrich Overbeck, Caspar David Friedrich, Max Liebermann, Lovis Corinth and Edvard Munch.

The **Burgkloster** vividly recreates the world of the Hanseatic traders.

Archaeological finds from Lübeck are displayed in the **Beichthaus** at the Burgkloster.

The list of museums and exhibitions in Lübeck doesn't stop there: the city also has the Museum of Nature and the Environment, the Völkerkundesammlung collection of ethnological items, the rotating exhibitions of the churches of Saint Catharine and Saint Peter, the 'History Workshop' accommodated in a former metal works and the Museum of Theatre Puppets, whose 20,000-plus articles from around the world captivate adults as well as children.

Culture in Lübeck also encompasses municipal theatre and opera at the stunning Jugendstil theatre, the municipal symphony orchestra, the Nordic film festival (featuring film productions from the Nordic countries), the many guest performances at the Music and Congress Centre, the Junge Oper (an experimental space for young operatic performers), the Youth Chamber Orchestra, the Media Docks (housed in a former dockside warehouse) and numerous small theatres.

Culture in Lübeck has many faces. The claim made at the start of this article is entirely justified: culture is not just a part of Lübeck – Lübeck is culture.

Anno Dominus providebit 1758

Durch den Roman „Buddenbrooks" von Thomas Mann weltberühmt geworden: Das Buddenbrookhaus

Gained worldwide fame following the novel "Buddenbrooks" by Thomas Mann: Buddenbrookhaus

Thomas und Heinrich Mann wohnten nicht im Buddenbrookhaus, waren dort aber bei der Großmutter zu Gast

Thomas and Heinrich Mann did not reside in Buddenbrookhaus, but frequently visited the house as their grandmother's guests

Mit dem Heinrich-und-Thomas-Mann-Zentrum wurde eine Forschungsstätte des literarischen Schaffens eingerichtet

The Heinrich-und-Thomas-Mann-Zentrum is a research centre for literary creativity

Schauplatz des Romans „Buddenbrooks" – eingerichtet, wie Thomas Mann die Räume beschrieb

Schönes muss man schützen: Auch bei den Buddenbrooks waren die Möbel verhängt

Things of beauty have to be protected: in the Buddenbrook household the furniture was covered with dust sheets

Setting of the novel "Buddenbrooks" – furnished as described by Thomas Mann

Ein Platz für Kinderträume: Das in „Buddenbrooks" beschriebene Figurentheater

A child's dreams come true: the puppet theatre as described in the novel "Buddenbrooks"

Riese unter den Türmen des Domes: In der Nähe von Lübeck gefundener Wal im Museum für Natur und Umwelt

A giant whale has found a home in the museum of natural history: the ancient skeleton was found near the city of Lübeck

Klassizismus in Vollendung: Fassaden in der Königstraße (in der Mitte das Museum Behnhaus)

Classicism shown to perfection: façades in Königstrasse (Behnhaus museum in the centre)

Ein Platz für die Kunst des 19. und des 20. Jahrhunderts: das Museum im Behnhaus (Königstraße 11)

A perfect display of art dating back to the 19th and 20th century Museum im Behnhaus (Königstrasse 11)

Die Mohren am Treppenaufgang brachte der Erbauer des Behnhauses aus Italien mit

The moors decorating the staircase were brought back from Italy by the first owner

Büste des Bürgermeisters Dr. Heinrich Behn, gegossen nach einer Marmorbüste von Fritz Behn

Bust of the mayor Dr. Heinrich Behn, cast on the basis of a marble bust created by Fritz Behn

Wohnkultur der Vergangenheit: Fayenceofen von 1773 der Manufaktur Stockelsdorf

Lifestyle of days gone by: Fayence stove dating back to 1773, produced by Manufaktur Stockelsdorf

Festsaal in einem früheren Privathaus: Kohpeis-Saal im Museum Drägerhaus (Königstraße 9)

Hall in a former private home: Kohpeis-Saal in Drägerhaus museum (Königstrasse 9)

So wohnten vermögende Bürger: Die Museen Behnhaus und Drägerhaus zeigen hervorragende Beispiele der Wohnkultur

The lifestyle of wealthy families: fine examples of sumptuous interiors are on display in the Behnhaus and Drägerhaus museums

Edvard Munch: „Die Söhne des Doktor Linde" (rechts); Oskar Kokoscka: „Sankt Jakobi" (unten)– Meisterwerke im Behnhaus

Edvard Munch: "The Sons of Doktor Linde" (right); Oskar Kokoschka: "Saint Jacob's" (below) – masterpieces shown in Behnhaus museum

In der Villa Eschenburg fand das Brahms-Institut sein Domizil

The Brahms Institute has found a home in Villa Eschenburg

Die ausdrucksstarke Farbigkeit der ursprünglichen Ausmalung konnte in der Villa Eschenburg erhalten werden

The vibrant colours of the original interior of Villa Eschenburg have been restored to perfection

Das Brahms-Institut der Lübecker Musikhochschule übernahm eine führende Rolle in der Brahmsforschung

The Brahms institute of the Lübeck College for Music played a pivotal role in the research into Brahm's work

Zeugnisse aus den Anfängen der Stadt im Kulturforum Burgkloster

Witnesses to the beginnings of the city shown in the Kulturforum Burgkloster

Hanseaten sind sparsam: Spardosen, die bei Ausgrabungen gefunden wurden

Hanseatic merchants are thrifty: money boxes found during excavation work

Die Geschichte der hansischen Kaufleute und des Geldes wird im Kulturforum Burgkloster erzählt

The history of Hanseatic merchants and the history of money is told in Kulturforum Burgkloster

Versteckt im Schatten der Petrikirche liegt das Museum für Puppentheater – das weltweit größte seiner Art

The Puppet museum nestles in the shade of St. Peter's Church – it is the largest museum of its kind worldwide

Marionetten und Handpuppen aus der ganzen Welt hat der Sammler Fritz Fey zusammengetragen

Fritz Fey has collected puppets from around the world

Handgeschnitzte Marionetten, etwa um 1900 gefertigt

Hand-carved puppets, made around 1900

Unentbehrlich im Puppentheater: Die Lustige Figur

Simply a must in every puppet show: Punch and Judy

Lübeck ist eine Einkaufsstadt für Individualisten

Designed to cater to individualists – Lübeck shops and boutiques

Verwirrend – und doch einfach: Das alte Straßennetz Lübecks hat sich nicht verändert (Stadtmodell im Museum Holstentor)

Confusing – yet so simple: the old Lübeck road system has not changed (model of the city displayed in Holstentor museum)

Kunst braucht Handel

„Mein Sohn, sey mit Lust bey den Geschäften bey Tage, aber mache nur solche, daß wir bey Nacht ruhig schlafen können." Diesen Rat ließ Thomas Mann in seinem Roman „Buddenbrooks" den alten Johann Buddenbrook an seine Nachkommen vermitteln. Es ist der Rat eines klugen Kaufmanns, der weiß, dass ein guter Leumund zu allen Zeiten die beste Voraussetzung für das nächste Geschäft ist. Zugleich versinnbildlicht dieser kleine Satz jenen Geist, der Lübeck prägt. Die Stadt verdankt ihr großes kulturelles Erbe dem Handel und dem Wagemut redlicher Kaufleute.

Art needs trade

"My son, show zeal for each day's affairs of business, but only for such that makes for a peaceful night's sleep." In the Thomas Mann novel 'Buddenbrooks', this is the advice that the ageing Johann Buddenbrook gives to his progeny. It is the advice of an astute tradesman who knows that a sound reputation has always been the best guarantee of survival in business. The statement also sums up the spirit that runs through Lübeck: the city owes its rich cultural heritage to commerce and the courage of honest merchants.

Wie zur Zeit der Hanse: Die Kraweel „Lisa von Lübeck" läuft aus

A reminder of the good old days of the Hanseatic League: the caravel "Lisa von Lübeck" leaves the port

Schiffsmodelle aus der Hansezeit im Museum Holstentor

Model ships dating back to the days of the Hanseatic League shown in Holstentor museum

Zum Nachzählen: Alle sieben Türme auf einem Foto

All towers accounted for: the proud number of seven caught in one photograph

Mit Salz wurde Lübeck reich: Die Salzspeicher neben dem Holstentor

White gold: the salt storehouses next to Holstentor have made Lübeck into a rich city

Auch einer Stadt können gelegentlich zwei Herzen in einer Brust schlagen. Merkur und Muse sind sich nicht unbedingt immer zugetan. Das Verhältnis zwischen Handel und Kultur ist häufig von Widersprüchlichkeiten geprägt. Lübeck macht da keine Ausnahme. Dennoch sind sich die Lübecker bewusst: Wirtschaft und Kultur bedingen einander. Das war zur Blütezeit der Hanse so, als der Handel künstlerische Werke von Weltrang finanzierte. Und das ist auch in der Gegenwart der Fall. Die Possehl-Stiftung (Possehl-Gruppe) und die Stiftung der Sparkasse zu Lübeck gehören heute zu den maßgeblichen Förderern von Kunst und Kultur in der Stadt. Damit bleibt eine gute Tradition lebendig. Der Erfolg der Kaufleute

Sometimes a city can serve two masters. Mercury, the god of commerce, is not necessarily compatible with the Muses. The relationship between commerce and culture is often one of contradiction, and in that respect Lübeck is no exception. However, the people of Lübeck know that business and culture thrive on one another. That's how it was at the height of the Hanseatic League, when it was business that financed world-class works of art; and that's how it is today, with the Possehl Foundation and the Sparkasse zu Lübeck Foundation ranking as two of the most significant sponsors of art and culture in the city. In providing their support, they are keeping a productive tradition alive: the success of the business community

Einst machten hier die Salzkähne aus Lüneburg fest: Auf Stadtrundfahrt vor den Salzspeichern

Former mooring place for salt barges from Lüneburg: a round trip of the city including salt storehouses

Unten am alten Hafen die Speicher und Kontore, oben auf dem Rücken der Stadtinsel die Gotteshäuser – das ist Lübeck

begründete den Erfolg der lübschen Politik, er schuf das Fundament für die Künstler und die Wissenschaft.

Dauerhaft erfolgreich kann der Handel nur gedeihen, wenn Friede herrscht. Die hansischen Kaufleute wussten das. In goldenen Buchstaben setzten sie den Leitspruch „Concordia domi – foris pax“ – „Eintracht im Hause – Friede vor den Toren“ auf das Holstentor, dem sicherlich bekanntesten Bauwerk der Stadt. Es entstand in der Zeit von 1464 bis 1478. Lübecks Geschichte war das anhaltende Streben, nach diesem Leitspruch zu handeln.

Der Gründung Lübecks durch Heinrich den Löwen im Jahr 1159 folgte bald die Blütezeit. Fast 300 Jahre lang führte Lübeck den Städte- und Handelsbund der Hanse, dem zeitweise 200 Mitglieder angehörten. Ihren Aufstieg zum Haupt des mächtigen Interessenverbandes verdankte die Stadt ihrer geographischen Lage sowie dem großen kaufmännischen und politischen Geschick ihrer Bürger. Im 12. Jahrhundert wendeten sich die Handelswege dem neu gegründeten Lübeck zu, denn die Stadt besaß als einzige weit und breit einen Ostseehafen. Dieser Hafen war das Tor zu den wichtigen Absatzgebieten Skandinaviens und Russlands. Der Aufstieg Lübecks begründete sich auf dem Handel mit Salz, Getreide, Fellen, Holz, Tuchen, Heringen und Stockfisch. All das wurde im Travehafen, dem Lebensnerv der Stadt, umgeschlagen. Später, als die Handelsreisen ausgedehnter wurden, entwickelte sich Lübeck zu einem bedeutenden

Häuser an der Obertrave

The storehouses and offices are scattered throughout the old port, whilst the skyline of the city isle is dominated by church spires – that's Lübeck

Houses on the banks of the River Obertrave

has always been a driving force behind local policy and laid the foundations for science and the arts.

The traders of the Hanseatic era also knew that business can only flourish in times of peace. They inscribed the motto "Concordia domi – foris pax" ("unity at home, peace abroad") in golden letters on the Holstentor gate, the most famous architectural symbol of the city, built between 1464 and 1478. The history of Lübeck is the history of endeavour to trade under that motto.

Lübeck was founded by Heinrich ('the Lion') in 1159 and immediately entered a period of prosperity. For nearly 300 years, the city dominated the Hanseatic League, the alliance of trading guilds that counted up to 200 members at times. The elevation of Lübeck to the head of the powerful coalition was down to its geographical location and the considerable commercial and political talents of its citizens. During the 12th century, trade routes converged on the new city of Lübeck, the only city for miles around with a Baltic port – the gateway to the major commercial regions of Scandinavia and Russia. Lübeck's rise to prominence was based on trade with salt, grain, animal hides, wood, fabrics, herring and dried cod – all of which passed through Trave harbour, the nerve centre of the town. Lübeck later became a major trading centre for red wine from France as the commercial routes grew longer. When Tsarina Catharine the Great appealed for settlers from Germany, for many emigrants the journey to the

Im Kaak von 1465 wurden Übeltäter an den Pranger gestellt, den Platz darunter nutzte man praktischerweise als Butterbude

In the Kaak, a place of execution dating back to 1465, culprits were placed in the stocks; the cellar was used as a storage area for butter

Handelsplatz für französischen Rotwein. Und als die Zarin Katharina die Große deutsche Siedler anwarb, da begann für viele Auswanderer in Lübeck die Reise ins russische Reich. Wenn heute auch keine großen Schiffe mehr im Hafen am Holstentor festmachen, andere Häfen sind weiterhin Lebensnerv der Stadt, vor allem der Nordlandkai und der Skandinavienkai mit regelmäßigen Verbindungen nach den skandinavischen und baltischen Ländern sowie nach Russland für Fracht und Passagiere. Lübeck-Schlutup hat sich zum bedeutenden Umschlagplatz für Papier entwickelt. Unter den deutschen Häfen an der Ostsee behauptet Lübeck seine führende Stellung.

Das unverwechselbare Stadtbild Lübecks entstand prägend während der Blütezeit der Hanse. Eng reihen sich die Giebel der nordischen Gotik aneinander, durchmischt von Fassaden der Renaissance, des Barocks und des Klassizismus. Viele der alten Häuser erzählen heute noch von den Kaufleuten, die sie einst

Neue Architektur in einer alten Stadt: Kaufhaus am Markt

New architecture in an old city: department store am Markt

Auch in einer Reichsfreien Stadt kommt ein Kaiser zu Ehren: Reiterdenkmal für Kaiser Wilhelm I

Although a free city in its own right, Lübeck honoured Wilhelm I by erecting a sculpture depicting the emperor on horseback

Russian empire began in Lübeck. Although large vessels no longer drop anchor at the port by the Holstentor, the city continues to revolve around its other harbours: the Nordlandkai and the Skandinavienkai in particular handle regular connections to the Scandinavian and Baltic states as well as freight and passenger traffic to Russia. Schlutup terminal has also developed into a major handling point for paper, helping Lübeck to retain its status as the leading German port on the Baltic coast. The unmistakable skyline of Lübeck was largely formed during the city's Hanseatic heyday. Northern Gothic gables crowd together, interspersed with Renaissance, Baroque and Classical façades. Many old houses continue to bear witness to the traders who once

Charakteristisch für eine windige Gegend: Windlöcher in der Fassade des Rathauses

Wind holes are a natural phenomenon in regions exposed to high winds

Zeichen eines selbstbewussten Bürgertums: Der neugotische Saal der Bürgerschaft von 1891

Decke im Rathaus (Bild oben); die Fassade der ehemaligen Börse (Bild unten)

Rathaus ceiling (above) and façade of the former stock exchange (below)

bewohnten. Die Kaufleute benötigten Lagerraum für ihre Waren. Dies Erfordernis bestimmte den Grundriss ihrer Häuser. Sie dienten als Speicher und boten zugleich Wohnraum. Die großen Dielen, die heute in ihrer architektonischen Großzügigkeit beeindrucken, waren von ihren Erbauern allein unter dem Gesichtspunkt der Zweckmäßigkeit angelegt worden. Sie mussten hoch sein, um möglichst viele Waren stapeln zu können. Erst vom 15. Jahrhundert an trennte man davon Wohnräume ab, die über eine Galerie zu erreichen waren.

Noch heute lässt sich an den Häusern Lübecks erkennen, in welchem Quartier die bedeutenden Fernhändler, die Krämer oder die Handwerker zuhause waren. So wird ein Gang durch die Stadt zur erlebten Geschichte. Und der Sozialgeschichte. Denn als Lübeck zur prosperierenden Handelsmetropole heranwuchs, da suchten immer mehr Menschen ihr Auskommen in der Stadt. Bald wurde es auf der Stadtinsel zwischen der Flüssen Trave und Wakenitz zu eng. Darum

Signs of a prosperous bourgeoisie: the House of the Burgher built in a New Gothic style in 1891

inhabited them. Traders needed somewhere to store their goods, and they addressed this need in the layout and design of their houses, which combined storage space with living space. The spacious hallways that strike us as generously proportioned today were built that way for reasons of practicality alone: ceilings needed to be high to accommodate as much stock as possible. It was only in the 15th century that living quarters were built separately and accessed via a gallery.

Even today, we can tell just by looking at the houses of Lübeck where the principal exporters, grocers and tradesmen lived. A stroll through the town therefore offers a living history as well as a social commentary. As Lübeck expanded into a thriving business capital and more and more people arrived to seek a livelihood in the city, the town on the island between the Trave and Wakenitz rivers quickly became overcrowded. That's when buildings started to be erected in the spaces behind the street-facing houses, giving rise to the narrow lanes lined with cramped dwellings known as

Audienzsaal des Rokoko im Rathaus (Bild oben); Renaissancetreppe am Rathaus (Bild unten)

Audience chamber in the town hall, built in a Rococo style (above) and Renaissance staircase (below)

Durchgang am Kanzleigebäude, darin arbeiteten seit dem 15. Jahrhundert die Kanzleischreiber des Rathauses

Passage leading to the chancellery, where clerks of the town hall have had their offices since the 15th century

begann man, die Flächen hinter den zur Straße ausgerichteten Häusern zu bebauen. Es entstanden die Gänge mit ihren Buden. So werden in Lübeck kleine Häuser genannt, in denen sich nicht mehr als eine Kleinstwohnung befindet. Die ersten Buden bestanden lediglich aus einem Raum mit einer offenen Herdstelle. Erst später wurde eine Aufteilung in Wohn- und Schlafraum vorgenommen und ein Stockwerk aufgesetzt. Damit war dann aus der Bude ein Ganghäuschen geworden. Der Weg in diese versteckte Welt der Gänge führt durch schmale Durchbrüche in den zur Straße ausgerichteten Häusern. 35 Prozent der Bevölkerung der Stadt lebten einst in 180 Gängen, einer Form des spätmittelalterlichen sozialen Wohnungsbaus.

Das herausragende Beispiel sozialen Engagements in Lübeck ist das Heiligen-Geist-Hospital, das als das älteste Altenheim der Welt gilt. Zugleich zählt es zu den wichtigsten Bauten der norddeutschen

'Buden'. The first Buden comprised nothing more than a room with an open stove. Later, the living quarters were divided from the sleeping areas and another level was added, turning the dwelling into a small lane house. This secret world of alleyways was reached via narrow cuttings in the houses that faced the road. At one time, 35 per cent of the town's population lived in 180 alleyways that resembled a kind of social housing scheme for the late Middle Ages.

The most striking example of social welfare in Lübeck was the Heiligen-Geist hospital, which can claim to be the world's first old people's home; it is also one of the most important surviving examples of the northern German Backstein Gothic style. The hospital, built in 1284 by order of the local authority, provided a refuge for elderly citizens and those in need of care. Beds were originally arranged side by side in a large hall with exposed roof beams, but eventually they were moved into separate 'cubbyholes'. These wooden closets

Auf dem Markt wird Tradition hochgehalten. Altes Handwerk findet immer Zuschauer und Käufer

In the market, traditions are upheld with pride. The old crafts are popular with onlookers and shoppers alike

Imposant in seiner gesamten Größe und auch im Detail: das Rathaus

Both its size and its attention to detail are impressive: the town hall

Die Gänge sind eine versteckte Welt für sich:
Sievers Thorweg Gang

The passages hold a very special charm:
Sievers Thorweg Gang

Die Gänge sind eine Form frühen Sozialen Wohnungsbaus: Petersilienstraße

The passages are examples of an early form of social housing: Petersilienstrasse

Eine hochherzige Stiftung aus dem Jahr 1639: Füchtingshof in der Glockengießerstraße

A generous endowment dating back to 1639: Füchtingshof in Glockengiesserstrasse

Seit mehr als 350 Jahren besteht die Stiftung des Johann Füchting unverändert fort

The Johann Füchting Foundation first established more than 350 years ago is still in existence

Backsteingotik. In dem 1284 im Auftrag des Rates gebauten Hospital fanden pflegebedürftige und alte Bürger eine Zuflucht. Ursprünglich stand in einer großen Halle unter freiliegendem Dachgebälk Bett an Bett. Später wurden die Schlafplätze in hölzerne Kammern von jeweils sechs Quadratmetern, die so genannten „Kabäuschen", aufgeteilt. Noch bis 1970 wurden diese Kammern genutzt.

Zu den bemerkenswerten sozialen Einrichtungen der Stadt zählen auch die vielen Stiftshöfe, Armen- und Elendshäuser. 170 davon gab es Ende des 19. Jahrhunderts. Jede dieser Einrichtungen setzte ein Zeichen hochherziger Hilfe, denn sie alle wurden aus Stiftungen vermögender Lübecker finanziert. Der Füchtingshof und der Glandorpshof, beide in der Glockengießerstraße, der Hasenhof in der Dr.-Julius-Leber-Straße und der Von-Höveln-Gang in der

measuring six square metres remained in use until as late as 1970.

The town provided other remarkable social facilities, including many shelters for widows and orphans as well as poorhouses and quarters for the needy. By the end of the 19th century there were 170 such refuges, each of

Lübecks Höfe und Gänge sind abgeschirmt vom Lärm der Stadt: Garbereiter Gang

The courtyards and passages of Lübeck are shielded from the noise of the city: Garbereiter Gang

Im ehemaligen Palais des Grafen Rantzau-Breitenburg arbeitet das Schleswig-Holstein Musik Festival

Wahmstraße sind beeindruckende Beispiele frühen sozialen Engagements. Hanseatischer Kaufmannsgeist und tätige Hilfe, beides verbindet sich in Lübeck überzeugend.

“Lubeke, aller Stede schone, van riker ere dragest du de Krone.” So reimte der Chronist Heinrich Rehbein im 16. Jahrhundert, ergriffen von der Schönheit der Stadt. Vermutlich hatte er dabei allerdings weniger das Gesamtkunstwerk im Sinn, das wir heute bewundern, sondern die prachtvollen öffentlichen Bauten der Stadt, die sakralen und die profanen. Wer von der Westseite kommend, etwa auf Höhe des Holstentores oder vom Malerwinkel, auf die Silhouette der Stadt blickt, wird die Begeisterung des Chronisten rasch verstehen. Hoch überragen die sieben Türme der Kirchen die Häuser auf der Stadtinsel.

The Schleswig-Holstein music festival has found a home in the former Count Rantzau-Breitenburg palace

which was financed by generous donations from wealthy Lübeck citizens as an act of compassion. Füchtingshof and Glandorpshof (both in Glockengiesser Strasse), Hasenhof at Dr.-Julius-Leber Strasse and Von-Höveln-Gang at Wahmstrasse stand as impressive examples of early social policy. In Lübeck, the Hanseatic spirit of commerce was effectively combined with hands-on aid.

In the 16th century, the chronicler Heinrich Rehbein was moved to proclaim that Lübeck “wore the crown as the most beautiful of towns”, so captivated was he by the city’s beauty. Presumably he was referring to Lübeck’s magnificent public buildings, both sacred and secular, rather than the synthesis of the arts that we can admire today. Anyone approaching the Holstentor city gate from the west or gazing from the Malerwinkel vantage point upon the city skyline, where seven

Blick aus der Kleinen Petersgrube auf die Ausstellungskirche St. Petri

St. Peter's Church as seen from Kleine Petersgrube

Vermutlich die älteste unter ihnen ist die St.-Petri-Kirche, die als erste Hallenkirche in Deutschland errichtet wurde. Heute wird sie nicht mehr als Kirche genutzt, dennoch aber besonders häufig besucht, denn in ihrem Turm befindet sich eine Aussichtsplattform, von der sich ein wunderbarer Blick über die ganze Stadt bietet.

Den Auftrag zum Bau des Domes, dem ehemaligen Bischofssitz, gab Heinrich der Löwe 1173. Es entstand eine romanische Basilika, die erst im späteren architektonischen Wettstreit mit der Kirche der Bürger, der Marienkirche, im Stil der Gotik ausgebaut wurde.

Die Kathedralen in Flandern und Nordfrankreich dienten als Vorbild für den Bau der Marienkirche, mit deren Bau um 1200 begonnen wurde. Die Ratskirche ist zum Inbegriff der norddeutschen Backsteingotik geworden.

Als Gotteshaus der Schiffer und Seeleute wurde die Jakobikirche erbaut, die 1227 erstmals urkundlich erwähnt wurde. Ein paar Schritte über die Straße, im Schatten des Turmes der Jakobikirche, steht die Schiffergesellschaft, das Amtshaus der Bruderschaft der Schiffer. Als „klassischste Kneipe der Welt" geführt, sitzen die Gäste heute noch an Tischen und auf Bänken, die bereits die Companienbrüder nutzten.

Die Aegidienkirche steht im ehemaligen Quartier der Handwerker und Ackerbauern. Als einzige der alten Stadtkirchen reiht sie sich nicht in die Linie der Gotteshäuser auf der Kuppe des Stadthügels ein. Erstmals erwähnt wurde die Aegidienkirche 1227. Im

Im Turm der St. Petrikirche befindet sich eine Aussichtsplattform

Observation platform in the tower of St. Peter's Church

church spires soar above the rooftops of the island, will quickly understand why Rehbein was so enchanted.

The oldest of the churches is thought to be the church of Saint Peter, the first hall church to be built in Germany. Although the structure no longer serves as a church, it still attracts large numbers of visitors, who climb the spire to a viewing platform that commands spectacular views across the city.

In 1173, Heinrich ('the Lion') ordered the construction of a cathedral for the Bishop of Lübeck. Originally built as a Romanesque basilica, it was subsequently converted into a Gothic-style building during a spate of architectural rivalry with St. Mary's, the people's church.

Inspired by the cathedrals of Flanders and northern France, construction of St. Mary's Church itself began in around 1200. The alderman's church epitomises the Backstein Gothic style of northern Germany.

The church of Saint Jacob, first documented in 1227, was built as a place of worship for sailors and mariners. Just over the road in the shadow of its spire is the Schiffergesellschaft, formerly the official headquarters of the brotherhood of mariners and today "the most classical eatery in the world". Guests can sit at the same tables and benches once used by the ship's company.

The church of Saint Aegidius stands in the former craftsmen's and farmers' quarter. It is the only one of the ancient city churches that is not aligned with the summit of the hill. The interior of the church, which was first documented in 1227, holds figurative Gothic and Renaissance paintings.

St. Jakobi war die Kirche der Seefahrer und Fischer. Die ältesten Zeugnisse stammen von 1227

St. Jacob was the patron saint of sailors and fishermen. The earliest pieces date back to 1227

Innern vereint sie figürliche Malereien der Gotik und der Renaissance.

Wenn auch die Türme der Kirchen alle anderen Bauwerke der alten Stadt überragen, Stolz und Selbstbewusstsein der Bürger versinnbildlicht das Rathaus. 1230 begannen die Lübecker ihr Rathaus zu bauen, und das Bauen nahm vorläufig kein Ende. Stets erwies sich das Rathaus als zu klein, stets musste es nach dem Geschmack der Zeit modernisiert werden. So mischen sich die Stile von Gotik, Renaissance und Neugotik zu einem der schönsten Rathäuser Deutschlands. Die Ratsherren Lübecks waren sich ihrer Bedeutung bewusst, schließlich war ihnen von höchster Autorität die Anrede „Ihr Herren" zuteil geworden. Mit diesen zwei Worten schmeichelte sich 1375 Kaiser Karl IV. bei seinem Besuch in die Herzen der Lübecker. Mit dieser Anrede verband sich die Einladung an die Lübecker, in den Rat des Kaisers zu kommen, „wann immer sie bei Hofe sind." Lübeck

Whilst the church spires rise above all other structures in the old town, the city hall embodies the pride and confidence of the citizens. The people of Lübeck started building their 'Rathaus' in 1230, and construction has never really been finished: the building continually turned out to be too small, or had to be modernised in keeping with the prevailing style of the age. As a result, its mix of Gothic, Renaissance and neo-Gothic styles have blended to form one of the most attractive city halls in Germany. The councillors of Lübeck were well aware of their own importance: they were even addressed as "My Gentlemen" by the highest of authorities, Emperor Charles IV. During a visit in 1375, the Emperor used these two words to ingratiate himself with the locals as he extended an invitation to "come and consult me whenever you happen to be at court". Alongside Rome, Venice, Pisa and Florence, Lübeck was one of the five cities whose representatives the Emperor referred to as "Gentlemen". It stands to reason, then, that the exceptional splendour of the city hall should reflect such a distinction.

In der Jakobikirche:
Altar (Bild oben); Epitaph für Sweder Hoyer von 1566 (kleines Bild rechts); Große Orgel (Bild unten). Seit 1467 sind in der Kirche zwei Orgeln belegt

The interior of St. Jacob's Church: Altar (above); epitaph for Sweder Hoyer dating back to 1566 (small picture to the right); large organ (below). Since 1467 the church has had two organs

Vor allem im Sommer ist Travemünde ein beliebtes Touristenziel. Jährlich werden 300.000 Übernachtungen gebucht

In summertime Travemünde is visited by many tourists. Anually 300.000 overnight-stays are booked

Die Travemünder Woche ist, nach Kiel, das größte Segelereignis der Welt

Travemünder Woche is beside the contest in Kiel one of the most famous sailing-attractions in the world

In Travemünde steht Deutschlands ältester, 31 Meter hoher Leuchtturm aus dem Jahre 1539 vor dem 1974 erbauten Maritim-Hotel

Germanies oldest Lighthouse from 1539 with a height of 31 meters is to find in front of the 1974 built Maritim-Hotel

Blick vom 119 Meter hohen Maritim-Hotel auf die Geschäftsstraße „Vorderreihe" in Travemünde

View from 119 meters high Martitim-Hotel down to the shopping-street "Vorderreihe" in Travemünde

Wenn der Fischer einmal nicht hinsieht:
Der Heringsdieb

Herring is popular fare, and when the fisherman has turned his back some try their luck

war neben Rom, Venedig, Pisa und Florenz eine der fünf Städte, deren Repräsentanten der Kaiser den Titel „Herren“ verlieh. Was Wunder also, wenn solcher Auszeichnung mit einem besonders prachtvollen Rathaus entsprochen wurde.

Mit dem Bewusstsein des reichen Erbes einer großen Vergangenheit ist Lübeck eine der Zukunft zugewandte Stadt. 5 500 junge Menschen studieren an der Medizinischen Universität, der Fachhochschule und der Musikhochschule. In einem zu den Media Docks umgebauten ehemaligen Hafenschuppen vermittelt die International School of New Media Studierenden umfassende Kenntnisse der Neuen Medien. Die in Lübeck beheimatete Drägerwerk AG, sie beschäftigt weltweit 10 000 Menschen, entwickelte sich durch wegweisende Innovationen

Lädt zum Promenieren ein:
Die Vorderreihe in Travemünde

Hat nach einer vorbildlichen Sanierung zum alten Glanz zurückgefunden: Hotel Grand SPA Resort A-ROSA

After painstaking restoration work, the hotel Grand SPA Resort A-ROSA has regained its old splendour

Whilst mindful of the rich heritage of its glorious past, Lübeck is a city that looks to the future. The University of Medicine, the University of Applied Sciences and the Academy of Music have a combined total of 5,500 young students. The International School of New Media, housed in a converted warehouse complex known as the Media Docks, offers students wide-ranging insights into the new media. Also based in Lübeck is Drägerwerk AG, a company with 10,000 employees world-wide; thanks to its pioneering innovations in the area of medical and safety technology, Drägerwerk AG has evolved into one of the leading companies in its field. The Possehl Group,

An ideal spot for a leisurely stroll: Vorderreihe shopping area in Travemünde

Wenn die Kunst auf Sand gebaut ist: Sand World in Travemünde

Art built on sand: Sand World in Travemünde

der Medizin- und Sicherheitstechnik zu einem der führenden Unternehmen auf diesem Sektor. Ebenso weltumspannend arbeitet die Possehl-Gruppe, deren Aktivitäten vom Erzkontor bis zur Fertigung von Reinigungsmaschinen reichen.

Der Tourismus ist in zunehmendem Maße eine der Säulen der Lübecker Wirtschaft. Die Stadt hat schließlich viel zu bieten: das einmalige Stadtbild und „die schönste Tochter". So nennen die Lübecker das Ostseebad Travemünde. Ferien in Travemünde – auch das hat eine lange Tradition. 1799 wurden die ersten Badekarren in das kühle Wasser der Ostsee gerollt, und von da an ging es aufwärts mit dem Fremdenverkehr. Hofräte, Dichter und Wirtschaftskapitäne entdeckten den Reiz des ältesten Bades an der Lübecker Bucht für sich. Seitdem ist „die schönste Tochter" immer schöner geworden. Die dicken Fährschiffe schieben direkt an den Nasen der Promenierenden vorbei. Die Viermastbark „Passat" fand ihren letzten Liegeplatz in

whose activities encompass everything from iron ore to the production of cleaning machines, is similarly globally active.

Tourism is increasingly important to the economy of Lübeck. The city has much to offer, including a unique townscape and a "beautiful daughter", as the people of Lübeck call the Baltic resort of Travemünde. The seaside holiday tradition of Travemünde goes back to 1799, when the first bathing machines rolled into the cool waters of the Baltic Sea. The tide of visitors has continued to rise ever since as councillors, poets and captains of industry have discovered for themselves the charm of the oldest resort on the Bay of Lübeck. During that time, the "beautiful daughter" has become even prettier. Hulking ferries glide past, almost within touching distance of people out for a stroll; the four-masted barque 'Passat' stands anchored in its final berth; the listed buildings of the casino and the spa rooms accommodate top-class hotels.

Spiel mit Licht und Wasser bei der Travemünder Woche

Play with light and water during a week's display in Travemünde

Die dicken Pötte fahren in Travemünde direkt an der Nase vorbei

Almost close enough to touch: barges in Travemünde

Ging in Travemünde auf Dauer vor Anker: Viermastbark „Passat“

The four-masted barque “Passat” has found a permanent mooring place in Travemünde

Reist mit seinen Seemannsliedern in alle Welt: der „Passat-Chor“ (Bild unten)

The “Passat” choir travels the world singing sea shanties (below)

Travemünde. In die denkmalgeschützten Bauten des Casinos und des Kurhauses zog eine Hotellerie der Spitzenklasse ein.

Vieles steht auf der Haben-Seite Lübecks. Doch besondere Schmankerln heben sich die meisten Menschen zum Nachtisch auf. Das soll bei diesen Porträtskizzen der Stadt Lübeck nicht anders sein. Genascht wird zum Schluss. Und was naschen die Lübecker so gerne wie deren Gäste? Selbstverständlich Marzipan. Als Stadt des Marzipans ist Lübeck weltbekannt, obgleich die orientalische Leckerei aus Zucker und Mandeln keineswegs in Lübeck erfunden wurde. Aber die Lübecker entwickelten bei der Herstellung eine besondere Kreativität. Und das seit mehr als 500 Jahren. Der gegenwärtig bekannteste aller Marzipanbäcker, das Unternehmen Niederegger, konnte 2006 den 200. Geburtstag feiern. Auch das ist ein Beispiel dafür, wie quicklebendig Tradition in Lübeck ist.

Für Besucher in Lübeck ein Muss: Konditorei Niederegger

Simply a must for visitors: Café-Konditorei Niederegger

Lübeck has other delicacies worth sampling. Just as the sweetest treats should always be saved for the dessert course, the same goes for this profile of Lübeck: the sweet comes at the end. So what kind of sweet do the citizens of Lübeck enjoy as much as visitors to their city? The answer, of course, is marzipan. Lübeck is renowned around the world as the city of marzipan. Even though the Oriental confection of sugar and almonds was invented far from here, the people of Lübeck have proved to be highly creative when making marzipan – for over 500 years. Niederegger, the best-known producer of marzipan, celebrated its 200th anniversary in 2006 – another example of the living tradition of Lübeck.

Lübecker Marzipan ist weltberühmt. Die Herstellung erfordert viel Sorgfalt

Marzipan from Lübeck is world-famous. The production of the almond sweetmeat requires great skill and care

Immer wieder eine Herausforderung an die Kreativität: Figurengruppe aus Marzipan

A real challenge: shaping a group of figures calls for exceptional creativity

Wohnen unter dem Turm der Aegidienkirche:
Eckhaus Aegidienstraße/ Schildstraße

*Living next to the tower of the church of St. Aegidius:
corner house at Aegidienstrasse/Schildstrasse*

Singechor von 1587, der Lettner ist ein Meisterwerk von Tönnies Evers

Singechor dating back to 1587, the rood screen is a true masterpiece created by Tönnies Evers

1227 wurde die Aegidienkirche erstmals erwähnt. Im 14. und 15. Jahrhundert wurde der Bau erweitert

The church of St. Aegidius was first mentioned in 1227. The building was extended during the 14th and the 15th century

Genau in der Mitte der Stadt, neben Rathaus und Markt, steht die Kirche der Bürger: Sankt Marien

The people's church of St. Mary's is situated in the very centre of the city, next to the town hall and the market square

Die Astronomische Uhr in St. Marien wurde im Zweiten Weltkrieg zerstört. Die jetzige Uhr baute der Uhrmachermeister Paul Behrens

The astronomic clock in the church of St. Mary's was destroyed during World War II. It was replaced by a new design created by master clock-maker Paul Behrens

Höher als alle anderen Türme im Abendland ragte die Turmspitze von St. Marien bei der Vollendung 1350

When completed in 1350, the church spire of St. Mary's was the highest in the Christian West

Eine Kathedrale von atemberaubender Schönheit: die Ratskirche Sankt Marien

The church of St. Mary's in all its breathtaking glory

Nach dem Vorbild der Kathedralen Flanderns und Frankreichs in Backstein gen Himmel gebaut: die Marienkirche

Following the designs of cathedrals in Flanders and France, St. Mary's Church was built in the Backstein Gothic style

Der Teufel wollte beim Bau der Marienkirche mitmischen. Nun sitzt er vor der Tür (Plastik von Rolf Goerler, 1999)

The devil himself wanted to lend a hand in the building of the church; he was given a place outside in the form of a sculpture created by Rolf Goerler in 1999

Gottes Lob, aus Backstein geformt:
Die Marienkirche ist gestalteter Bürgerstolz

Built for the higher glory of God: St. Mary's Church, witness to the pride of Lübeck's burghers

Der Dom war die Kirche der Bischöfe – und musste am Rande der Stadt gebaut werden

The cathedral was the church of the bishops – it had to be built outside the city

Der Lettner trennte Chor und Gemeinderaum. Er entstand zur gleichen Zeit wie das Triumphkreuz

The rood screen divided the choir from the congregation. It was created at the same time as the cross of triumph

1477 wurde das Triumphkreuz von Bernt Notke im Dom errichtet. Den Auftrag erteilte Bischof Albert Krummedieck

The cross of triumph by Bernt Notke was erected in the cathedral in 1477. It was created by the order of bishop Albert Krummedieck

Von weither sind die charakteristischen Doppeltürme sichtbar: Blick auf den Dom

View of the cathedral: the characteristic twin towers can be seen from afar

Einer der wichtigsten Bauten norddeutscher Backsteingotik: Das Heiligen-Geist-Hospital von 1284

One of the most important examples of the North German Backstein Gothic style: Heiligen-Geist-Hospital dating back to 1284

Vermögende Kaufleute spendeten das Geld, mit dem das Heiligen-Geist-Hospital gebaut werden konnte

The money for the Heiligen-Geist-Hospital was donated by wealthy merchants of the city

Für bedürftige Bürger gegründet, ist das Heiligen-Geist-Hospital bis heute ein Altenheim

Founded for the needy, the Heiligen-Geist-Hospital has been turned into a retirement home

Die so genannten „Kabäuschen" im Heiligen-Geist-Hospital dienten bis 1970 als Altenwohnungen

Up to 1970, the small box-like rooms in the Heiligen-Geist-Hospital were used as self-contained apartments for the residents of the retirement home

1335 wurde der Grundstein für das Katharinenkloster des Franziskanerordens gelegt. Es bestand bis zur Reformation

The foundation stone for the monastery of St. Catherine's of the Order of St. Francis was laid in 1335. The latter existed until the reformation

Figurengruppe von Ernst Barlach an der Westfront der Katharinenkirche: Frau im Wind – Bettler – Sänger

Group of figures by Ernst Barlach in the west front of the church St. Catherine: Woman in the Wind – Beggar – Singer

Prinzessin Elya aus der Sankt-Jürgen-Gruppe (1498), Replik in der Museumskirche St. Katharinen

Princess Elya as part of the Group of St. George (1498). Replica in the church of St. Catherine's (museum)

Sankt-Jürgen-Gruppe, von Bernt Notke für die Nikolaikirche in Stockholm geschnitzt. In Lübeck steht eine Replik

The Group of St. George was created by Bernt Notke for St. Nicholas Church in Stockholm. The group shown in Lübeck is a replica

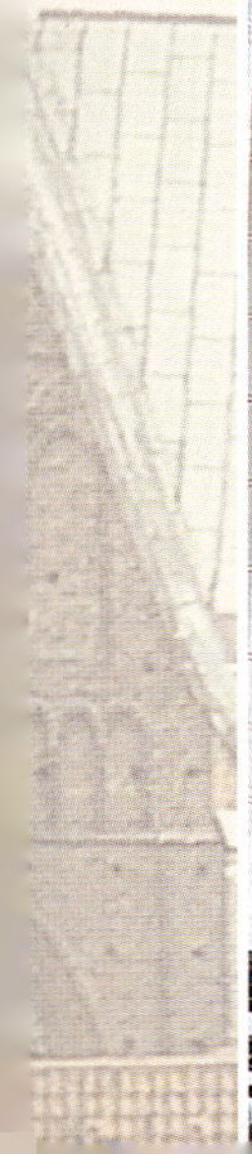

Mönchsempore in der Katharinenkirche. Das erste Kloster der Franziskaner in Lübeck wurde bereits 1225 gebaut

The monk's gallery in the church of St. Catherine's. The first Franciscan monastery in Lübeck was built as early as 1225

Im Scharbausaal der Stadtbibliothek schliefen einst die Mönche des Katharinenklosters

The Scharbausaal of the city library once served as sleeping quarters for monks of the monastery of St. Catherine's

Das Psalterium gehört zu den Kostbarkeiten der Stadtbibliothek

The psalter ranks among the most treasured possessions of the library

Aus der Schatzkammer der Stadtbibliothek: Miniatur des Erfurter Buchmalers Johannes Falkenstein

From the treasury of the city library: a miniature created by the Erfurt artist Johannes Falkenstein

Durch das Burgtor kamen die Bauern aus Mecklenburg in die Stadt

Farmers from Mecklenburg entered the city through Burgtor

Ehemaliger Schwurgerichtssaal im Komplex des Burgklosters

Former court room in the complex of the Burgkloster

Im Burgkloster: Halle im Nordflügel (oben), Wandmalerei in der Sakristei (Mitte), Kapitelsaal (unten)

Burgkloster: hall in the north wing (above), wall painting in the vestry (centre), chapter hall (below)

Gewölbeausmalung in der Sakristei, Gewölbeschlussstein mit Wappen

Vault painting in the vestry; knot with coat of arms

Eine Fassade im Stil der niederländischen Renaissance: Kanzleigebäude

A façade in the style of the Dutch Renaissance: the building of the chancellery

ZONE
Lieferverkehr frei v. 5-10.30 h u. 19-22 h
Radfahrer von 19-9 h frei

Das Feuerschiff „Fehmarnbelt“ hat seinen letzten Liegeplatz gegenüber der Mengstraße

The lightship “Fehmarnbelt” has found its permanent mooring place opposite Mengstrasse

Ein winterlicher Morgen im Langen Lohberg

A wintry morning in Langer Lohberg

Hoffentlich sind es nur erfreuliche Nachrichten:
Post für die Lichte Querstraße

*Hopefully all the news is good news:
mail for Lichte Querstrasse*

Wenn der Abend kommt, wird es still in der Stadt

Once the sun has set, the sounds of the city begin to fade

debitel

Ein Platz für Träume von Fernweh:
Kai an der Untertrave

*Just the place for dreaming of faraway places:
quay on the River Untertrave*

Lübecker über Kultur und Leben in Lübeck

Beruflich pendele ich regelmäßig zwischen Hamburg und Lübeck. Ich freue mich jedes Mal aufs Neue, wenn ich entweder mit dem Zug oder mit dem Auto die wunderschöne Lübecker Altstadt erreiche. Schon vor der Ankunft im Zentrum stimmen die sieben Türme auf die Schönheit der Hansestadt ein. Nach Erreichen der Innenstadt noch die Trave überqueren, das Holstentor passieren und bei St. Petri abbiegen und schon habe ich die Zielgerade vor mir: die Parade mit dem Sitz des Schleswig-Holstein Musik Festivals, das seit Mai 2005 im wundervollen Palais Rantzau residiert – wer hat schon eine solch schöne Anfahrt und einen Arbeitsplatz, der unsere Mitarbeiter und Besucher gleichermaßen berauscht.

Rolf Beck,
Intendant des Schleswig-Holstein Musik Festivals

Life and culture in Lübeck

My job involves commuting between Hamburg and Lübeck on a regular basis. No matter how often I make the trip, by train or car, I always look forward to reaching the delightful old town of Lübeck. As I approach my destination, the seven church spires remind me of the beauty of this Hanseatic city. When I come into the centre of town, I cross the River Trave, pass the Holstentor city gate and turn off at the church of Saint Peter. Then I'm in the home straight: the Parade, home of the Schleswig-Holstein Music Festival, which took up residence in the magnificent Palais Rantzau in May 2005. Few people can boast such an enjoyable journey to work, not to mention a place of work that captivates staff and visitors alike.

Rolf Beck,
Director of the Schleswig-Holstein Music Festival

Der Oldtimerhafen lädt zum Bummeln und zum Bewundern ein

The port for old-timers is ideal to take a stroll or admire the craftsmanship of days gone by

Warum ich mich in meiner Heimatstadt Lübeck so wohl fühle? Meine Antwort: Die Stadt ist mit ihrer lebendigen Kulturlandschaft immer wieder Inspiration, Anregung und Ausgleich – für mich persönlich sowie für meine Familie, Freunde und Geschäftspartner. Lübeck bietet eine abwechslungsreiche Palette kultureller Einrichtungen auf einem hochkarätigen Niveau und ist damit kultureller Anziehungspunkt über die Grenzen Deutschlands hinaus. Ob Mehrspartentheater, die Museen mit ihren vielfältigen Ausstellungen, die Musikhochschule oder das Schleswig-Holstein Musik Festival: Das reiche Erbe Lübecks wird durch das Engagement ihrer Bürger – jung und alt – immer wieder zum Leben erweckt und läuft damit nicht Gefahr, sich auf der Auszeichnung Weltkulturerbe auszuruhen. Nur so lässt sich der kulturelle Reichtum unserer Stadt bewahren.

Dr. Christian Dräger,
stellvertretender Aufsichtsratsvorsitzender
Drägerwerk AG

People sometimes ask me what it is I like about my home town of Lübeck. I tell them that thanks to its vibrant cultural scene, the city is a constant source of inspiration, stimulation and equilibrium – not just for me personally, but for my family, friends and business partners. With its wide range of illustrious cultural facilities, Lübeck attracts culture-seeking visitors from well beyond the borders of Germany. However, it is the dedicated citizens of all ages who continually revitalise the rich legacy of Lübeck: from the multi-purpose theatres to museums with ever-evolving exhibitions, from the Academy of Music to the Schleswig-Holstein Music Festival. Despite having been declared a World Heritage Site, the city refuses to rest on its laurels. In this way, we can preserve the cultural treasures of our city.

Dr. Christian Dräger,
Deputy Chairman of the Supervisory Board,
Drägerwerk AG

Schnee verzaubert das Quartier der Stecknitzfahrer

A winter wonderland: The quarters of the Stecknitz canal crews

In Lübeck geboren, zog ich nach dem Abitur in die „weite Welt". Stationen waren u.a. London, Berlin, Baden-Baden und Hamburg. Warum ich hierher zurückkam? Lübeck hat was.

Überschaubar genug für ein Gefühl des Dazu-Gehörens – und groß genug, um sich auch heraus zu halten. Nicht metropolenhaft hastig und überdreht. In der Innenstadt ist alles bequem zu Fuß zu erreichen, und das Meer liegt in unmittelbarer Nähe. Freie Wahl: Mitmachen im öffentlichen Betrieb oder in Ruhe gelassen werden? Alles jederzeit möglich. Angebote gibt es genug. Und wenn ich mal die Walkabouts sehen will oder Mark Knopfler, bin ich in einer Stunde in Hamburg. Und dann setz ich mich wieder ans Wasser und guck auf die Trave.

Wolfram Eicke, Autor, schreibt Bücher und Musicals, u.a. „Der kleine Tag" und „Das silberne Segel"

I was born in Lübeck, but went off to see the big wide world after taking my school-leaving examinations. Having travelled to London, Berlin, Baden-Baden, Hamburg and other places, why did I come back to Lübeck? There's just something about the place.

The city is small enough to promote a sense of belonging, yet big enough to retain your privacy. The hectic tension of a metropolis is absent. The attractions of the city centre are comfortably negotiated on foot, and the sea is close by. Participate in the public bustle, or find your own space – it's your choice. There's plenty going on, all of the time. If I want to see a band like the Walkabouts or Mark Knopfler, I can be in Hamburg in one hour. Then I can sit by the water and gaze at the Trave.

Wolfram Eicke, author of books and musicals including "Der kleine Tag" and "Das silberne Segel"

Auslaufen in Travemünde: Nimm mich mit Kapitän auf die Reise…

Leaving the port of Travemünde: a life on the ocean wave, a home on the rolling deep...

„Travemünde allein mit seinen Herrlichkeiten war die ganze Reise wert, und ewig wird der Anblick des Meeres meiner Seele vorschweben.“

Joseph von Eichendorff, 1805

“The splendour of Travemünde alone made the whole journey worthwhile. I will always carry the aspect of the sea in my soul.”

Joseph von Eichendorff, 1805

Wieder einen großen Pott raus gebracht: Der Lotse kehrt zurück

Another barge on the way: the pilot boat has returned

Wenn Sand zu leuchten beginnt: Farbspiele bei der Sand World

The fascination of sand: beautiful colours at Sand World

Logenplatz mit komplettem Lübeck-Panorama: Radisson-Hotel an der Trave

A truly spectacular view of Lübeck: Radisson-Hotel on the River Trave

Finanziell besehen liegt Lübeck, dereinst „Königin der Hanse", ganz unköniglich darnieder; die Bewegungsmöglichkeiten der Stadt sind extrem begrenzt – und kurzfristige Änderung kaum zu erwarten. Wo also liegen die Pfunde, mit denen sich wuchern lässt, wo die Reichtümer, die dem Nutzen und Frommen der Stadt dienstbar zu machen sind?

Neben einigen großen, renommierten und einer wachsenden Zahl junger, innovativer Unternehmen, neben dem florierenden Hafen und einer beachtlichen Hochschullandschaft (Universität und Fachhochschulen) ist es zuvörderst die Kultur, sind es die vielfältigen kulturellen Angebote, die Lübecks Attraktivität begründen.

Das historische Stadtbild mit seinen architektonischen Glanzlichtern, allen voran die backsteingotischen Kirchen; die Museenlandschaft nebst den Literatur- und Nobelpreisträger-Häusern; das Theater und die fabelhafte Philharmonie; die renommierte Musikhochschule; dazu zahlreiche private Spielstätten und der Kunstverein: Das alles fügt sich zu einer ästhetischen Palette, die den wohl größten Reichtum der Stadt darstellt. Diesen kulturellen Schatz zu pflegen und zu befördern ist erste städtische wie auch Bürgerpflicht.

Björn Engholm, Ministerpräsident a. D.

Lübeck, at one time the 'Queen of the Hanseatic League', has ended up anything but regal from a financial point of view; the city's chances of upward mobility are severely limited, and change is highly unlikely in the short term. Where is the inspiration that will drive prosperity, where are the riches of which the city can avail itself?

On the plus side, the city can point to several large, high-profile corporations and a growing number of young and innovative companies; the port area is booming; and Lübeck is home to some impressive higher education institutions. First and foremost, however, it is the broad range of diverse cultural facilities that makes the city an attractive place to be.

The historical cityscape is packed with architectural highlights, principal among which are the Backstein Gothic style churches, the museums, the houses of literary and Nobel Prize winners, the theatre and the superb philharmonic orchestra, the prestigious Academy of Music, numerous private venues and the art association. All of this adds up to a cultural wealth that is surely the city's greatest asset. Upholding and promoting this aesthetic heritage is our primary municipal and civic duty.

Björn Engholm, former Minister President

Versteckt unter dem Hang der Traveböschung liegt die Fischersiedlung Gothmund

The houses of the fishing community of Gothmund are nestled along the embankment of the River Trave

Die Fischer von Gothmund besaßen die Fischereirechte bis an die Ostsee

The fishermen of Gothmund held the fishing rights for an area reaching up to the Baltic Sea

Mit dem Namen Hansestadt Lübeck verbindet sich nicht nur eine Stadt der Wirtschaft, sondern auch der Wissenschaft und Kultur. Als Lübecker bin ich stolz auf dieses Ambiente, denn Kunst und Wissenschaft gelten heute mehr denn je als Reservoir persönlicher Freiheit, und das macht sie für die Gestaltung unseres Lebens so wertvoll.

Als Leistungsträger in diesem Sinne wirken neben den vielen Vereinen und Gesellschaften vor allem die Medizinische Universität, die Technische Fachhochschule, die Musikhochschule, die Theater, Museen, Bibliotheken, die Galerien, die Musik- und Kongreßhalle und das hansestädtische Archiv, alles Einrichtungen und Institutionen, deren wissenschaftliche und kulturelle Ausstrahlung weit über Lübeck hinausreicht.

Gleiches gilt für die Persönlichkeiten aus allen Bereichen des Kultur- und Geisteslebens, die den Namen „Lübeck" in alle Welt getragen haben.

Die Brüder Thomas und Heinrich Mann, Günter Grass, Emanuel Geibel, Gustav Falke, Buxtehude, Tunder, Johann Sebastian Bach und Händel, Abendroth und Furtwängler, Dohnanyi, Albrecht und Klee, Erich Ponto, Jürgen Fehling, Günther Lüders und Horst Frank. Sie alle haben mit ihrem Wirken dazu beigetragen, das ich auf Lübeck als Stadt der Kultur stolz bin.

Dr. Robert Knüppel,
Geschäftsführer Deutsche Stiftung Denkmalschutz,
Bürgermeister a. D.

Eines der ältesten Häuser Lübecks:
Hier übernachtete 1375 die Frau des Kaisers Karl IV.
Der Herrscher schlief im Nachbarhaus

One of the oldest houses in Lübeck: this is where the wife of Charles IV broke the journey for the night in 1375. The sovereign was accommodated in the house next door

The Hanseatic city of Lübeck is associated not just with commerce but also with science and culture. As a native of Lübeck, I am proud of the city's reputation. After all, more than ever before, it is art and science providing the source of personal freedom that plays such a vital role in changing our lives.

Alongside the many societies and associations, the key players in achieving this are the University of Medicine, the University of Applied Sciences, the Academy of Music, the theatre, museums, libraries, galleries, the Music and Congress Centre and the Hanseatic City Archive – facilities and institutions whose scientific and cultural prominence is acknowledged far beyond Lübeck.

The same recognition is extended to the personalities from all fields of the city's cultural and spiritual life who have carried the name of Lübeck around the globe.

The brothers Thomas and Heinrich Mann, Günter Grass, Emanuel Geibel, Gustav Falke, Buxtehude, Tunder, Johann Sebastian Bach and Händel, Abendroth and Furtwängler, Dohnanyi, Albrecht and Klee, Erich Ponto, Jürgen Fehling, Günther Lüders and Horst Frank: all have played their part in making Lübeck the city of culture in which I take pride.

Dr. Robert Knüppel,
Managing Director, German Foundation for the Protection of Monuments, former mayor

Auf Pirschgang im Quartier der Stecknitzfahrer

Stalking in the quarters of the Stecknitz canal crews

Lübeck, die Musikstadt, in der ich lebe und arbeite.

Die sieben Türme der fünf Altstadtkirchen im Weltkulturerbe, Buxtehude – Bach – Distler ----- Der Verein der Musikfreunde, Musikkultur seit 1896 ----- Das Jugendstiltheater, Oper und Orchester, weltberühmte Dirigenten ----- Die Brüder Mann und die Musik, Aufbruch in die Moderne ----- Schleswig-Holstein Musik Festival, eine Bürgerinitiative geht um die Welt ----- Die Musikhochschule in Schleswig-Holstein, 41 Nationen in 22 denkmalgeschützten Häusern, der Blick in die Zukunft.

Prof. Jörg Linowitzki,
stellv. Rektor der Musikhochschule,
Vors. Verein der Musikfreunde

Lübeck, the musical city where I live and work.

The seven spires of the five churches in Lübeck's old town, a World Heritage Site: Buxtehude-Bach-Distler ----- The Society of the Friends of Music: Musical culture since 1896 ----- The Jugendstil theatre, opera and orchestra: World-renowned conductors ----- The Mann brothers and the music: Emergence of a modern age ----- The Schleswig-Holstein Music Festival: A people's initiative with global reach ----- The Academy of Music in Schleswig-Holstein, 41 nations in 22 listed buildings, looking to the future.

Professor Jörg Linowitzki,
Deputy Rector of the Academy of Music,
Chairman of the Society of the
Friends of Music

Für Autos wurden die engen Straßen in der Altstadt nicht geplant

The old part of Lübeck does not cater for modern traffic

„Es ist mein Ehrgeiz, nachzuweisen, daß Lübeck als Stadt, als Stadtbild und Stadtcharakter, als Landschaft, Sprache, Architektur durchaus nicht nur in Buddenbrooks, deren unverleugneten Hintergrund es bildet, seine Rolle spielt, sondern daß es von Anfang bis Ende meiner ganzen Schriftstellerei zu finden ist, sie entscheidend bestimmt und beherrscht."

Thomas Mann, 1926

"My aim is to demonstrate that Lübeck – the city, the townscape, its character, its landscape, language and architecture – has played a pivotal part not only in Buddenbrooks, to which it undeniably forms the backdrop, but in my entire body of work, from start to finish; this town defines and guides my writing."

Thomas Mann, 1926

Klein, aber für viele Besucher die wichtigste Verbindung zur Stadt: Die hölzerne Brücke über die Trave

Small but vital for many visitors to the town: the wooden bridge across the River Trave

Die Leitlinie „Zukunft Lübeck" sieht zu Recht in der Hansestadt die Kulturstadt des Nordens; denn die vielseitigen kulturellen Aktivitäten der Denkmalpflege, der neuen Kulturstiftung der Stadt mit ihren 11 Museen, der Musikhochschule, des Theaters und der Oper, aber auch der vielseitigen Künstler der bildenden Kunst und Literatur prägen in zunehmendem Maße nicht nur das Erscheinungsbild der Stadt, sondern sind zu einem wichtigen wirtschaftlichen Faktor geworden. Nicht zuletzt aus diesem Grunde fördern auch eine Mehrzahl Lübecker Stiftungen die gemeinsamen Anstrengungen, den Anspruch Lübecks als Kulturstadt des Nordens nachhaltig zu rechtfertigen.

Dr. Helmuth Pfeifer,
Vorsitzender Possehl-Stiftung

The 'Future of Lübeck' vision rightly regards the Hanseatic city as the centre of culture for the north. To an increasing degree, the city's image is defined by the energetic preservation of historical monuments, the city's new cultural foundation, the 11 museums, the Academy of Music, the theatre and the opera, not to mention the many creative individuals working in the fields of fine arts and literature. These multifaceted cultural activities have also emerged as a critical economic factor. For this reason, amongst others, many foundations in Lübeck are working together to secure Lübeck's long-term position as the cultural city of the north.

Dr. Helmuth Pfeifer,
Chairman of the Possehl Foundation

Abendliche Stimmung am Rande der Altstadt. Die Lichter spiegeln sich in der Trave

Dusk creeping in from the outskirts of the Altstadt. The lights are reflected in the River Trave

C.A.FISCHER & SOHN

Neues und Altes miteinander in Harmonie zu verbinden ist für Lübeck ein bleibender Auftrag

To blend the new and the old in perfect harmony is a permanent matter of concern for the city of Lübeck

Gespräche mit Besuchern unserer altehrwürdigen Hansestadt machen immer wieder deutlich, dass der Aufenthalt in Lübeck häufig als eine Art Museumsbesuch erlebt wird – Backsteingotik, Buddenbrooks und Kirchenmusik.

Die Verengung der vorherrschenden Sichtweise auf die herausragenden Zeugnisse der Vergangenheit wird der Breite des kulturellen Spektrums in unserer Stadt nicht gerecht. Kultur ist für mich ein Spannungsbogen zwischen Altem und Neuem, sowohl in der Architektur, der bildenden Kunst, der Musik, im Theater und in der Literatur.

Neugier auf Neuartiges und nicht zuletzt die Bereitschaft, auch für Impulse aus

When I meet visitors to our venerable Hanseatic city, they often tell me that staying in Lübeck is like staying in a museum dedicated to Backstein Gothic, Buddenbrooks and church music.

The narrowness of this prevailing view, which focuses on the heritage of a glorious past, does not account for the breadth of our city's cultural spectrum. For me, culture is like an arc of dramatic tension connecting the old and the new – in architecture, the fine arts, music, theatre and literature.

A thirst for the new – and an openness to influences from other cultures – are signs of a vibrant society.

"Die Fremden" – Thomas Schütte's group of four 'outsiders' on the roof of the Music and

Nach der Stadtgründung wurde in Lübeck der Baugrund knapp: Man sieht es

Once the city had been founded, land was worth their weight in gold – for obvious reasons

anderen Kulturkreisen offen zu sein, kennzeichnet eine lebendige Gesellschaft.

„Die Fremden" – die vier Figuren auf dem Dach der MuK – von Thomas Schütte, gemahnen uns, Menschen, die selbst eine reiche kulturelle Tradition besitzen, nicht an einem Ort verharren zu lassen, an dessen kulturellem Programm sie nicht teilhaben. Integration – auch das ist Ausdruck von Kultur.

Wolfgang Pötschke,
Vorstand Sparkasse zu Lübeck AG

Congress Centre – remind us that people with their own rich cultural traditions cannot remain tied to a place where they take no part in cultural life. Integration is another manifestation of culture.

Wolfgang Pötschke,
Chief Executive, Sparkasse zu Lübeck AG

Spielerischer Ausdruck des Bürgerstolzes: Turmreihe am Rathaus

Looked at with pride by the citizens of Lübeck: the intricate towers of the town hall

Winter, Wakenitz und Lübeck – das ist perfekt

Winter, the River Wakenitz and Lübeck – a striking combination

Lübeck ist für mich <u>die</u> Stadt der Kultur!

Sie bietet eine Vielfalt, die ihresgleichen sucht…

Alleine dieses „Meer“ aus Backstein in unserer schönen Altstadt lässt uns bei einem Rundgang den Geist der damaligen Zeit spüren.

Wundervolle Patrizierhäuser und einmalige Baudenkmäler aus Renaissance, Barock und Klassizismus, eingebettet in Wasser und Grün, sind ein Gesamtkunstwerk. Tag für Tag erfreue ich mich an meiner Stadt – einer der schönsten Städte des Nordens!

Peter Sünnenwold, Stadtpräsident

As far as I'm concerned, Lübeck is <u>the</u> city of culture, a city with a unique diversity!

As you walk around our charming old town, the abundance of Backstein buildings regenerates the spirit of a bygone age.

Magnificent patrician houses and unique, historically important buildings dating from the Renaissance, Baroque and Classical periods amount to a synthesis of the arts set against a backdrop of water and greenery. This is one of the most beautiful cities in the north of Germany, and a place I enjoy to the full every day!

Peter Sünnenwold, City President

Transitorium der Universität zu Lübeck. Im Vordergrund eine Plastik von Gerhard Backschat

Transitorium of Lübeck University. In the foreground a sculpture by Gerhard Backschat

Aus der Medizinischen Akademie (gegründet 1964) wurde die Universität zu Lübeck

Lübeck University evolved from the Medical Academy (established in 1964)

Jniversität und Iochschulen machen übeck zur jungen tadt

Jniversity and colleges dd a touch of youthful ibrancy to Lübeck

Das Magische Auge wacht über das Uni-Gelände

The magic eye watches over the University campus

Wo geht es denn hier lang? Bronzeguss des Stadtmodells auf dem Markt

Where do I find... model of the city cast in bronze, found in the market square

Verzaubern die Stadt zur Winterzeit: Figuren der Ice World

Adding a touch of winter magic to the city: Ice World figures

Besucher der Ice World müssen sich warm anziehen

Visitors of Ice World have to dress warmly

Winterspaziergang an der Obertrave

Stroll along the banks of the River Obertrave

Die großen Fernhändler der Hansezeit wohnten in der Mengstraße

During the period of the Hanse, prosperous traders had their residences in Mengstrasse

Das Schabbelhaus in der Mengstraße geht auf eine Stiftung für lübsche Wohnkultur zurück

Schabbelhaus restaurant in Mengstrasse is a fine example of Lübeck lifestyle

Wohnkultur und Esskultur verbinden sich im Schabbelhaus

Schabbelhaus offers a very special kind of lifestyle

Die junge, neue Welt der Informationstechnologie in den Media Docks…

The new and innovative world of IT has found a home in the Media Docks...

… und die alte Welt der Pastorenhäuser am Koberg versinnbildlichen Lübecks Spannungspole

… and the old world of the vicarages on Koberg bears witness to days gone by

Lübecks Welt ist Backstein: Der Dom, das Zeughaus und das Gesellenhaus

In Lübeck intricate brickwork reigns supreme: the Dom, the Zeughaus and the Gesellen-haus

Ein passender Rastplatz für eine Möwe

Just the right place for a seagull

Reich beschnitzte Haustür im Zopf-stil des ausge-henden Rokoko

Richly carved de-corations depict-ing the braided design of the late Rococo period

In der Stadt der Giebel finden sich immer neue Formen und Varianten

The city of gables proudly presents an overwhelming variety of the most intricate designs

Neogotik, Klassizismus und Renaissance vereinen sich zu einem Bild

The styles of Neo-Gothic, Classicism and Renaissance merge to create perfect unity

Türen und Portale gaben erste Auskunft über die Bewohner eine Hauses

Doors and portals offer initial information on the occupants of the dwelling

Ein wahrhaft krönender Abschluss eines Giebels

A gable crowned in magnificent perfection

Die Schiffergesellschaft – die „klassischste Kneipe der Welt“ – ist das einzige in Lübeck erhaltene Amtshaus

Schiffergesellschaft – a pub and restaurant steeped in tradition. It is the last Amtshaus in Lübeck

Auf den alten Bänken der Nowgorod-, Schonen- und Bergenfahrer sitzen heute die Gäste

Guests now occupy the old benches of vessels that once travelled to Novgorod, Schonen and Bergen

Das beeindruckende Rokoko-Portal der Schiffergesellschaft stammt aus dem Jahr 1768

The impressive Rococo portal of the Schiffergesellschaft house dates back to the year 1768

Es ist nicht immer einfach, die berühmten Gänge und Höfe in der Lübecker Altstadt zu erreichen

Sometimes it is difficult to reach the famous passages and courts

Blicke vom Maritim, Travemünde *Views from Maritim, Travemünde*